ABOUT MY GRANDP

 This Is Grandpa

His name: _____

How I call him _____

His age: _____

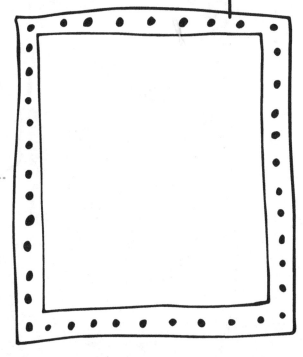

Our favorite thing to do together is

....

....

LOVE AND SPOIL

This is what

GRANDPA

Is all about

I love hearing stories about

....

....

Grandpa And Me Drawing

I love you because you tell me I am

....

....

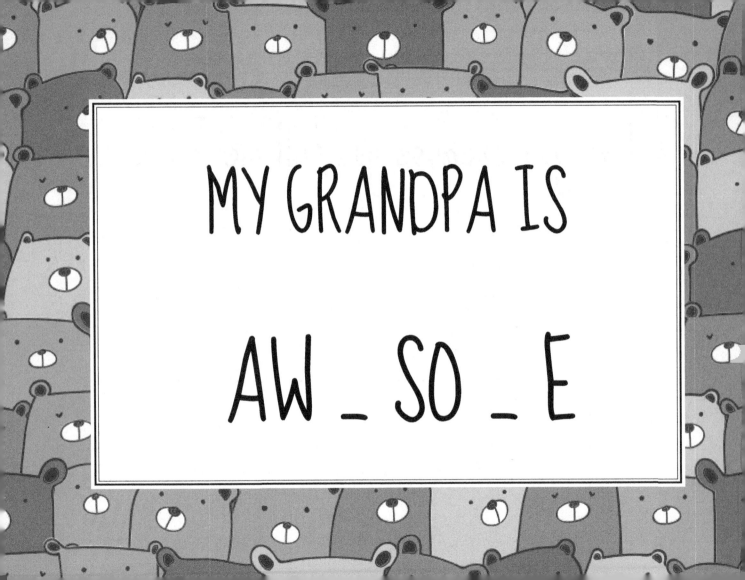

I love it when we play

....

....

I love the way you give the best
advice when

....

....

My favorite place in your house is

....

....

I was so happy when you made me a

....

....

DADDY

knows a lot

but **GRANDPA**

knows everything

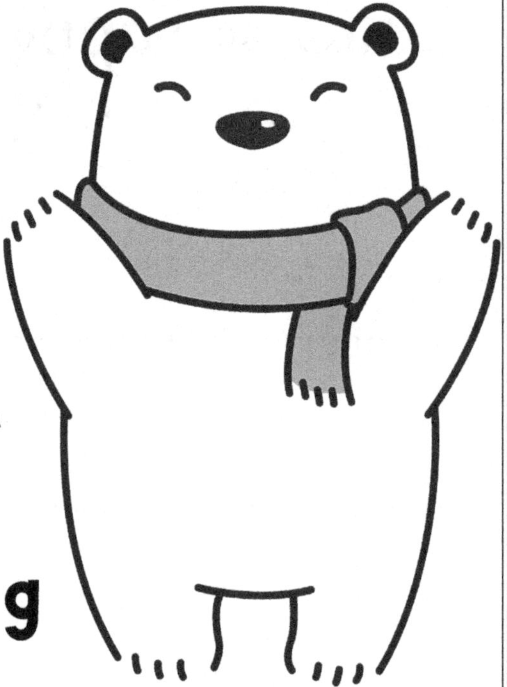

I love that you taught me

....

....

This is Grandpa in three words:

*

Everyone knows that you are

....

....

You are so funny when

....

....

You deserve the

....

....

Award

I will always cherish that day when

....

....

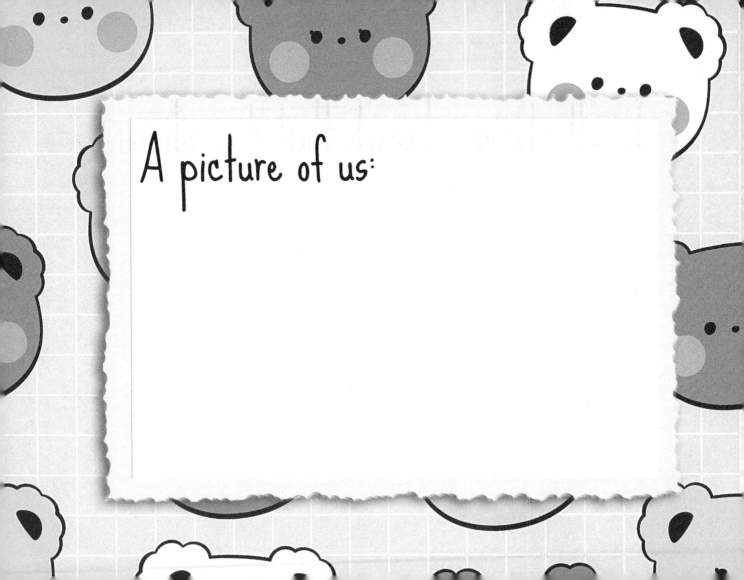

A picture of us:

I love you because you can

....

....

faster than anyone

I love you because you can fix

....

....

I drew this picture for you, Grandpa

I would like to learn more about

....

....

My favorite place to go with you is

....

....

Grandpa, you make the good moments better and the hard ones

easier

I remember when you

....

....

I would definitely like to do this

with you again

You are very good at

....

....

The most amazing thing we have done together is

....

....

I know you are the happiest when

....

....

This is Grandpa

By Me

I love the way you cheer when I

....

....

This is Me

By Me

If I could get you anything in the world, it would be

....

....

Together we make the absolute best

....

....

TEAM

When we are apart, it makes me
happy to think about

....

....

I Love You,
GRANDPA
You Are
The Best

I know you love me because

....

....

The most important thing I learned from you is

....

....

I am really grateful for

....

....

"Every day is special when I get to spend it with my Grandpa."

You are the best
Grandpa ever because

....

....

Want FREEBIES?

Email Us At:

larasvows@gmail.com

Title the email "What I Love About Grandpa For Kids"
and let us know that you purchased our book.

_____

THANKS FOR YOUR AMAZING SUPPORT!

>>>>>>>>>>>>>>>>>>>>>>>>>>>>>>

For Enquiries and Customer Service
email us at:

larasvows@gmail.com

We don't exist without you. A brief review could help us a lot. Please leave your feedback about this book.

SCAN THE OR CODE BELLOW

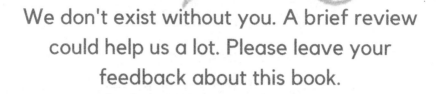

>>>>>>>>>>>>>>>>>>>>>>>>>>>>>>>>>>>

THANKS FOR YOUR AMAZING SUPPORT!

Made in the USA
Las Vegas, NV
07 December 2024

13484616R00037